The U.S. Character Deficit And How to Restore it

One Individual at a Time Through the Power of Wisdom

Table of Contents

Introduction

Chapter 1 - *What is Character and does it Matter* -------------------------------------- 9

Chapter 2 - *Your Character Pyramid* -- 18

Chapter 3 - *The True North of a Nation* -- 24

Chapter 4 - *What is Truth* --------------- 29

Chapter 5 - *True North of American Values* -------------------------------------- 33

Chapter 6 - *True North of Secular America* ---------------------------------- 35

Chapter 7 - *Truth in your True North* -- 38

Chapter 8 - *What is Wisdom* ----------- 44

Chapter 9 – *Knowledge and Wisdom of Self* ------------------------------------- 67

Chapter 10 - *Building Your Character Pyramid* ---------------------------------- 72

Appendix 1 ------------------------------- 74

Introduction

When I think of the greatest Leader of Character in American history, I think reverently of George Washington. I was never interested in history until the past few years when I began to feel our country being threatened from within to lose its greatness. I started studying the life of George Washington and his role in founding our country. I realized how selfless and humble he was, knowing it was not his personal greatness, but the greatness of an entire nation of people standing beside him to fight for what was good and right in the eyes of God. These men who chose George Washington as their top military general and first President of their new United States swore in their Declaration of Independence, their lives, their fortunes and their sacred honor, to regain their God-given rights and freedoms that were being taken from them.

Today, we are at another critical juncture in our nation's history. Like the Founders and those who stood with them opposing the tyrannical treatment of English rule, we too are facing tyrannical treatment from *our* elected leaders. They are disregarding the Declaration of Independence and the Constitution of the United States that the Founders created, the states ratified, and the people laid down their lives to defend. The Founders were God-fearing people who understood that power corrupts, so they crafted a form of government never before tried by a nation, in which the people rule themselves through elected representation and the rule of law. They devised a balance of power that would not allow any one person or group of people to gain too much power that would lead to corruption. George Washington is one individual in our history who dealt responsibly with power and knew that even he should not be granted the power of a king, lest the same fate come upon future generations. Over the past 200 years, from the humility and wisdom of our Founders who risked everything they had to start again as a new nation, the United States of America has become the most prosperous and free nation on earth. I contend that it was the character of our Founders and the framework of character they devised in our system of government *of the people, by the people, and for the people*, that built our great country to what it is. And it is the breakdown of this framework of character that is threatening the existence of our country as we have known it.

Why is there a deficit of character in our country today? I contend that if people do not have a clear *Purpose* in life, with meaning and value based on a defined set of principles and values, they will wander through life looking for other people and things to fill their void with whatever *feels* good. They seek change but don't really understand what change they want. They follow their feelings and ideals for a better future, but they don't examine the course they intend to venture down.

I teach my children that if _you_ don't take control of your life, _someone else will_. _You_ must direct your life or you are going to be directed _by others_. _You_ must remain vigilant to protect the freedoms you have been given by God, and to guard against others who seek to control your life. If you don't have an opinion about something, someone else will give you his. If you don't take a firm stand for your values and principles, someone else will replace them with hers. Be vigilant and scrutinize where information comes from, whom you follow, and what you believe. And help your family and friends do the same. Other people with lesser character would love to get ahold of your mind and your passion, and steer them in a direction that is consistent with their character. It is therefore important to know your *Self*, the *World* around you, and your *guiding values and principles* in life, and to gain *Wisdom* in a practical and personal way that leads to a higher *Purpose* and meaning in life. This is the make-up of your *Character Pyramid* that we will examine in this book. How solid and true is your foundation of knowledge in *Self*, the *World*, and your guiding values and principles? Can you see clearly the practical and personal nature of *Wisdom* in your life as it relates to you, others and your guiding values and principles? Does *Truth* and *Wisdom* lead you to a clear and meaningful *Purpose* in life, that you can articulate and defend, so no one will move you and others in your life anywhere but the direction you choose?

Analyzing Your Character Pyramid will give you the clarity you need to weather any storm and attain any level of success you aspire to. As a *bonus for purchasing this e-book*, you will receive access to an online talent assessments (a $250 value) to build your personal Character Pyramid and help others in your life do the same. We already have the framework of character our Founders left us in our Declaration of Independence and Constitution. Too many Americans have lost their way and gone over the *character cliff. We the People* need to resume our original course. Let us shore up our own Character Pyramid, and then help our family and friends do the same, to regain our standing as the strongest and most generous and prosperous nation on earth. Let us be proud of and understand the meaning and purpose of our American Character Pyramid, depicted on the back of every American dollar bill, and known as The Great Seal of the United States of America. And let us create our own Character Pyramid as a seal of great personal *strength of character* in our own lives.

Chapter 1: What is Character and does it matter

From as early as I can remember, I learned from my parents and my conscience to never tell a lie. Maybe that is why I respect and relate to George Washington as much as I do. We grew up learning that George Washington never told a lie. The tale of him chopping down the cherry tree might have been in our elementary school history books, but not in anything I've read by credible historians as an adult. So I'm wondering now if that story was an attempt to create a shadow of skepticism around his stellar character and leave a questionable impression in our young minds. That line of thinking would otherwise sound like a conspiracy theory and a thought the *left* would want us to feel uncomfortable saying, but look around at what has become acceptable behavior by our supposed leaders of character today in politics, business, the military, and even the clergy. There is plenty of justification to be suspect about what has been influencing us in America as individuals and as a nation. We must look at our educators, media, television, movies, music and today's interactive video games for children and adults. When we do examine these areas, is there any wonder for the ethical confusion about right and wrong; good and evil; character and corruption?

Recently in the news, Jeffrey Immelt, Chairman and CEO of General Electric, a $150 billion corporation said about China, "State-run communism may not be your cup of tea, but their government works." I assume, then, state-run communism *is his* cup of tea since he is praising it. Would he prefer to implement communist/socialist values and principles in the United States and within GE that are completely counter to the U.S. Constitution, Declaration of Independence, and free market capitalism? Is Jeffery Immelt the 21st Century Leader of Character whom we are supposed to rally behind? Do the 280,000 GE employees have any choice but to rally behind their leader of character? What does this say about the character of the GE organization? Is GE a corporate leader of character for all American corporations?

What about Supreme Court Justice Ruth Bader Ginsburg who said in reference to the Egyptian revolution of 2012, "I would not look to the U.S. Constitution if I were drafting a constitution in the year 2012." Is she a 21st Century Leader of Character, appointed by President Clinton and confirmed by the United States Senate, as 1 of 9 Supreme Court Justices who swear to support and defend the Constitution of the United States, and bear true faith and allegiance to the same?

And what about President Clinton himself who looked directly into the camera and lied to each one of us watching, stating "I did not have sexual relations with that woman, Ms. Lewinski," when in fact he later admitted to a grand jury that he did? Is he a 21st Century Leader of Character and was he upholding the character of the office of Presidency of the United States of America by bringing a 23 year old intern into the oval office to have oral sex, which we now know is what he did?

And former CIA Director and retired 4-star General David Petraeus, whom many thought was the consummate Leader of Character, but whom we now know was having an extramarital affair, and risking national security of the United States, with inappropriate and sex-related email communication, with the female co-author of the David Petraeus biography *All In*? Is David Petraeus the 21st Century Leader of Character we are all to rally behind?

I could go on-and-on and I'm sure you could too. When I think about these examples of high level and supposed leaders of character in our country today, it is clear to me there is ethical confusion and a deficit of character among leaders in politics, business, media, entertainment, and all levels of education, most notably our colleges and universities.

A major concern I have today is that you and I (assuming you agree with me on the character deficit in our country), may soon come to a tipping point in our nation's history, where the majority who believe in traditional American Values of the Declaration of Independence and Constitution, are displaced by a loud minority of dissenting American leaders, and their *peloton* (to use a bicycle road racing analogy) of large groups of Americans drafting behind the leaders, using little energy of their own to gain momentum and consume the field.

I go back to the question about why anyone would want us to believe as young children in elementary school, that George Washington was anything but a great leader of character?   I believe it has everything to do with what character *is*. According to the Merriam-Webster dictionary, character is *the complex of mental and ethical traits marking and often individualizing a person, group, or nation*.

The mental and ethical traits I use, and I believe most conservatives including our Founding Fathers, use to determine someone's level of character are *honesty, integrity, liberty, justice, individual prosperity and self-control*. But what if another group of Americans use *knowledge, power, control, social justice, interdependence, fairness and equality* as the mental and ethical traits that *mark and individualize great leaders of character*? Would a leader of character look differently to these two groups of people? I believe leaders like George Washington, Thomas Jefferson, Abraham Lincoln and Ronald Reagan would be in the first group, while Woodrow Wilson, Bill and Hillary Clinton, Al Gore and Barrack Obama would be in the second group. I am quite sure the leaders in Group 1 would not consider the leaders in Group 2 to be great leaders of character, and I believe there would be similar opposition by the leaders in Group 2 to characterizing Group 1 as great leaders of character. Again, the distinction as a leader of character lies in the mental and ethical character traits that define the individual, group or nation. America as a nation, in order to agree on the character of the nation and of its people, must have a common definition for the mental and ethical traits (the character) of the nation, and the good that the nation brings to the rest of the world, and to the individuals who comprise it.

Dr. Robert S. Hartman was a Nobel Prize nominee and psychologist born in WWI Germany, and lived in WWII Nazi Germany in his early 20's. He was appalled at his countrymen's blind nationalism and loyalty to a clearly evil leader in Hitler and the Nazi party that carried out Hitler's vision of ethical character. Dr. Hartman, having left behind his real name, Robert Schirokauer, and the life he was born into, fled Nazi Germany to the United States and dedicated the rest of his life to understanding how good people like his father, uncles, and his own brother could believe such evil was good. He was nominated for the Nobel Prize just before his death in 1973, for developing the *Science of Formal Axiology,* which is the science of how we think and make decisions. This science is the first and only science able to consistently and accurately measure value (good and bad) in ethics and philosophy, through scientific and mathematical correlations. Like natural sciences, born of correlations in math with the forces of nature, we are now able, through math and science, to measure how we value what is good and bad, and how that value pattern leads to predictable human behavior and decision making. If Dr. Hartman did a study on the structure of value between Group 1 and Group 2 leaders mentioned previously, he would identify a distinctly different value pattern between groups. In their own estimation, each is right and good because they value differently, but according to the science of value, there is a distinct formula and *hierarchy of value* for positive and negative valuations. In formal axiology, *opposing values cannot both be good*. So here we have a value science that delivers a clear definition of good and evil and the shades of grey in between.

In formal axiology, *good* is defined by an axiom (the root of axiology). The axiom of good is satisfied by anything that fulfills the concept, or defining properties of a person, thing or idea. A *good* chair for example, has all the characteristics of a chair including a platform with three or more legs, to evenly and stably support the full weight of a person. A bad chair does not fulfill the properties of a chair, so it may have 2 legs, or no platform, or supports unevenly, or is unstable. According to Dr. Hartman's definition of good, you can be a good thief, or a good murderer, if you fulfill the concept of a thief or murderer. Good, is therefore not necessarily morally or ethically good, but fulfills all the properties of the subject.

This explains the variance in perspective about good character in the two groups of leaders. Group 1 defines good character as *honesty, integrity, liberty, justice, individual prosperity and self-control*. Group 2 defines good character as *knowledge, power, control, social justice, interdependence, fairness and equality*. If a leader fulfills all of the properties of *Group 1 character*, he is a good leader of character. He may however demonstrate bad character to supporters of *Group 2,* because he does not fulfill their concept of character, including *knowledge, power, control, social justice, interdependence, fairness and equality*.

Similarly, a good leader of character from Group 2, demonstrates *knowledge, power, control, social justice, interdependence, fairness and equality,* but they are seen to exhibit bad character to Group 1 supporters, if they do not demonstrate *honesty, integrity, liberty, justice, individual prosperity and self-control*.

When we talk about the character of a nation, group or individual, are we therefore unjustified in saying that one group is right and the other is wrong? It appears in our nation today that we are nearly split down the middle between Group 1 and Group 2, and each is pointing to the other as wrong and themselves as right. Since America is a democracy (it is actually a Republic), should the majority decide which group should prevail and establish the one consistent definition of good character for our people and our nation? In essence, is that what we should accept, when we democratically elect our leaders in a national election of President and Representatives in Congress?

Chapter 2: The Character Pyramid

I contend there are three facets to the character of an individual, group or nation. Those are *Truth*, *Wisdom*, and *True North*. *Truth* and *Wisdom* form the *framework* of the Character Pyramid. *Truth* is the *foundation* and *Wisdom* is the superstructure. *True North* provides direction as your *guiding values and principles*. *True North* is the leading edge and one of three anchor points of the Character Pyramid (Figure 1).

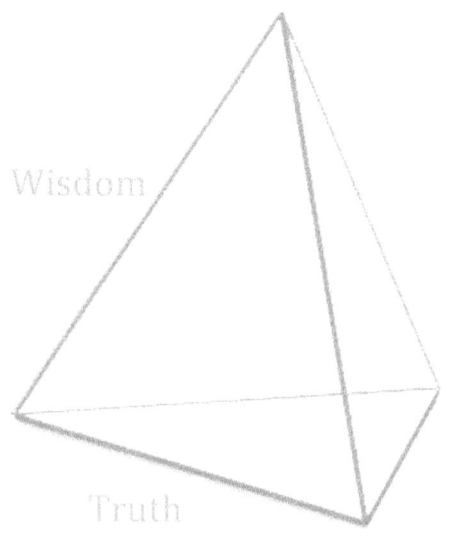

Figure 1

The other two anchor points are your *Self* and the *World* (Figure 2). *Self* represents everything *within you*, and the *World* represents everything *outside of you*, including your spouse, family, friends, business, community, nation, world and everything in it.

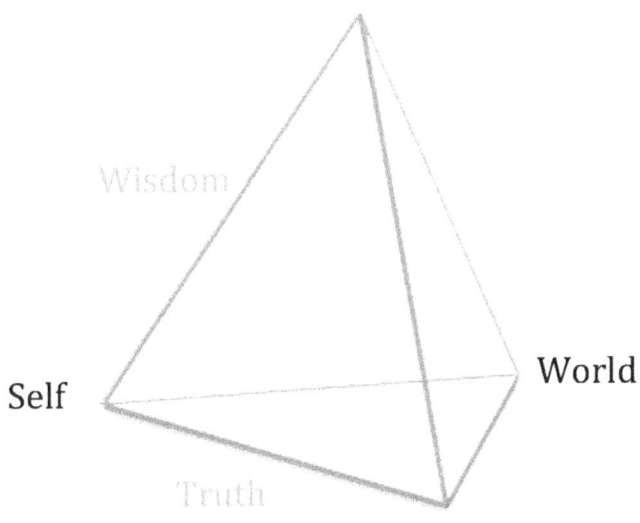

Figure 2

The Character Pyramid now depicts a framework of *Truth* and *Wisdom* interconnecting your *Self*, *True North*, and the *World* (Figure 3). Your *Purpose* in life, represented by the top point of the pyramid, arises from *Truth* and *Wisdom* of your *True North*, *Self* and the *World*. Each will be explored in greater depth throughout the book.

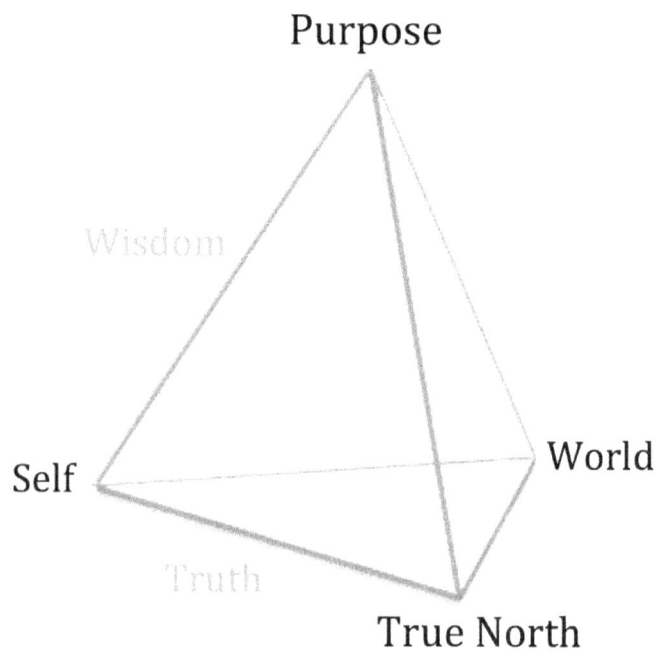

Figure 3

Without any one of the three facets of *Truth*, *Wisdom* and *True North*, the character of an individual, group or nation is compromised.

Without *Wisdom,* we have no substance. There is only knowledge, which has little value on its own (Figure 4).

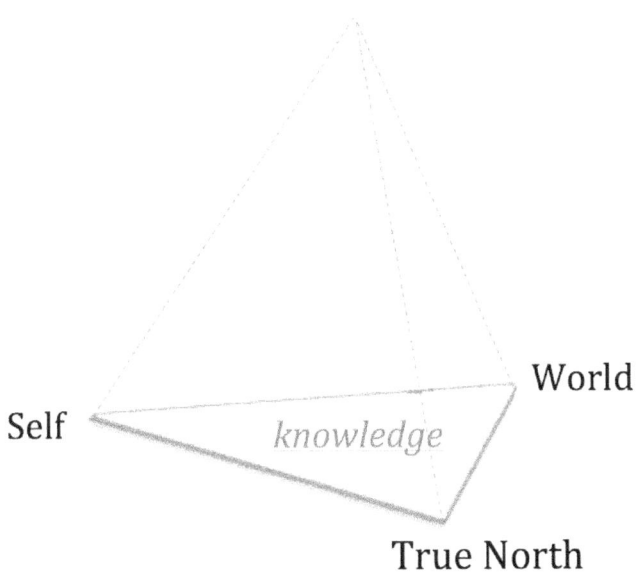

Figure 4

Without *Truth*, we cannot have *Wisdom* or *knowledge,* and we lose touch with our *Self, True North* and the *World* around us.

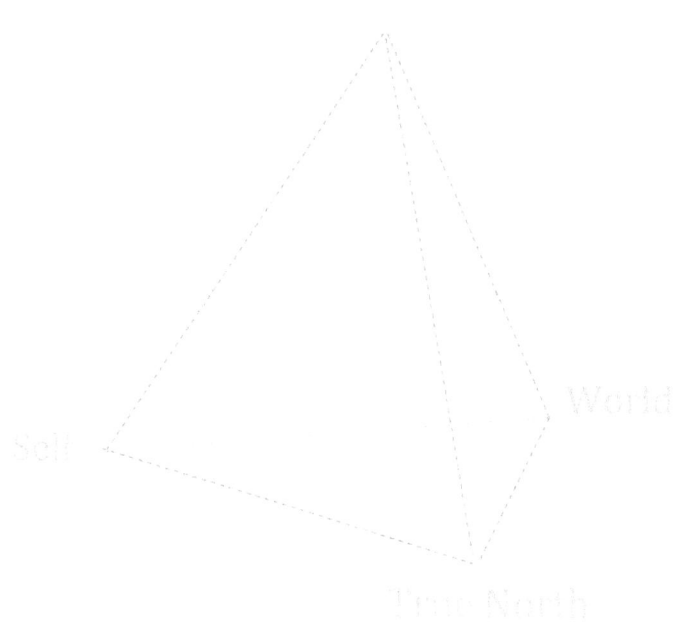

And without *True North* we have no anchor and reference point to guide us in life. *True North* is therefore the starting point for building the foundation and framework for a strong Character Pyramid.

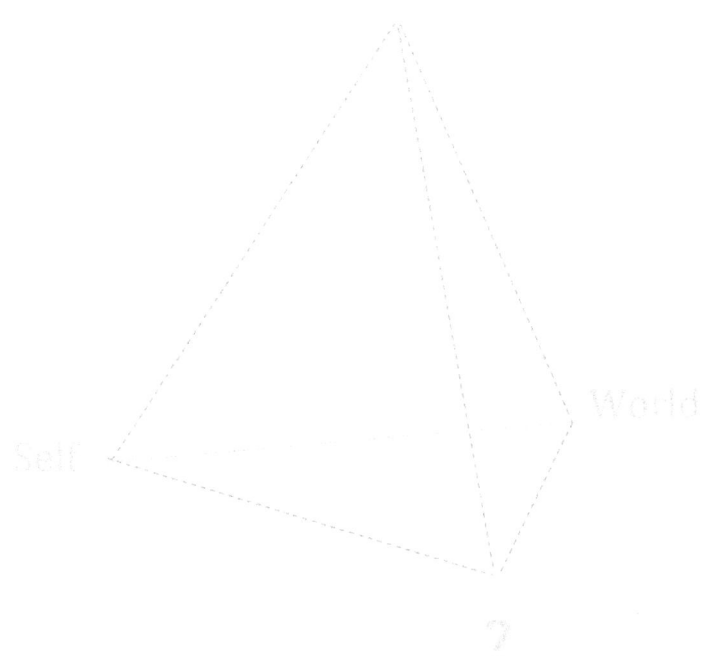

Chapter 3: The True North of a Nation

The *True North* of a nation (its guiding values and principles) comes from the *True North* of the sum of its parts. In other words the *True North* of the individuals and groups that make up a nation becomes the *True North* of the nation.

The *True North* of American colonists at the founding of America in the late 1700's was heavily influence by Judeo-Christian values and principles. Most of the Founding Fathers were Christian believers who lived by the principles and values of the Bible. Even those who were not Christians or Jews, but agnostic, deist, or atheist, studied the Bible and understood and appreciated the *Truth*, *Wisdom* and *logic* of the Bible regarding right and wrong, good and evil.

It is clear that the Founding Fathers incorporated their biblical values, into the drafting of the Declaration of Independence and United States Constitution. Following are passages from the Declaration that reference God:

*When in the Course of human events, it becomes necessary for one people to dissolve the political bands which have connected them with another, and to assume among the powers of the earth, the separate and equal station to which the **Laws of Nature and of Nature's God** entitle them, a decent respect to the opinions of mankind requires that they should declare the causes which impel them to the separation.*

*We hold these truths to be self-evident, that all men are created equal, that they are **endowed by their Creator** with certain unalienable Rights, that among these are Life, Liberty and the pursuit of Happiness.*

*And for the support of this Declaration, **with a firm reliance on the protection of Divine Providence**, we mutually pledge to each other our Lives, our Fortunes and our Sacred Honor.*

The Founders devised a system of government that had never before been adopted or even considered by a nation. They believed they were guided by the hand of Divine Providence when drafting these documents that divided the governing body and created a balance of power so no one person or group could gain too much power, leading to corruption and tyranny. Drafted in the U.S. Constitution and Bill of Rights are the rights and freedoms granted to individual Americans by God, and irrevocable by man, with *power of the people* to elect their governing officials, and *rights* to protect themselves, their property, and their freedoms, against all enemies foreign and domestic. The Declaration of Independence and Constitution of the United States of America therefore became the guiding values and principles for a new nation, the *True North* of America.

Over the past 100 years or more, there has been an attack by the left wing of the world, and within the United States, on traditional American values, the American *True North*. I am convinced those who hold values counter to traditional American Values expressed in the Declaration of Independence and Constitution of the United States, are a relatively small but loud minority of Americans, but whom would have us believe they are the majority. These are leaders of the Group 2 category discussed in Chapter 1, with mental and ethical character traits that include *knowledge, power, control, social justice, interdependence, fairness and equality*. These are the Immelts, Ginburgs, Gores, Clintons and Obamas of today's politics and business. And they have been the leaders of choice for large numbers of Americans in recent years. This loud minority of leaders are hijacking the American Character from large groups of Americans (by race, class and gender) who ultimately establish the character of our nation. If the loud minority is successful in overturning the character of enough individuals and groups in our country, they will have succeeded in changing the American Character that made us the most prosperous and powerful source for good in the world.

A threat to the American Character is a real threat to the character of your community, church, business, and ultimately a threat to your family and individual character. The strategy of leftism is to divide and conquer, and when applied to the character of a nation, a split character is a nation divided.

As responsible American citizens our first duty is to our family, which includes our *Self*. Our family and our *Self* is also where the rebuilding of our character as a nation must begin. We need to examine our own Character Pyramid, starting with *Truth* in our own *True North*. What is the source of your personal and family values and principles? Is knowledge of *Self*, the *World* and your *True North*, supported by *Truth* and *Wisdom*? Do you have a clear *Purpose* that naturally emits from the *Truth* and *Wisdom*, of your personal and family Character Pyramid? The following chapters will further develop the facets of your personal Character Pyramid, which naturally and exponentially translates into restoring the American Character Pyramid.

Chapter 4: What is Truth

Where do you go to find truth today? Do you read it in the newspaper, or listen to it on the evening news, CNN or Fox News? Do you find it in talk radio, from books you read, or did you learn it from teachers in school? We have often been told, "Don't believe everything you hear," but how do we know what is the truth and what is not? Often leaders in politics, business, the military, school and church tell us their perspective on the truth, and then we find other "credible" leaders and sources in the same field with completely contrary "truths". To ensure your Character Pyramid has a firm foundation in *Truth*, you must first establish your source of *True North*.

If you use a compass to navigate, North on the compass is not necessarily the real, or *True North*. A compass generally points north from the magnetism of the earth's rotation, but there is a slight or significant variance between Magnetic North and *True North*, depending where you are in the world. There may be no visual or apparent factors to indicate you are off course, but without compensation for *True North*, you will wander further and further off course, following a course you *think* is true. You must however, make a course correction to arrive at your desired destination. We use the *True North* metaphor for our journey in life because if we try to navigate life without a compass and without our *True North* to give us proper course corrections, we will never arrive at our desired destination or the significant points along the way.

I was a helicopter pilot in the Army and one of the idioms they pounded into our heads in flight school was, "believe your instruments". If we tried to go inside ourselves and navigate, or *fly by the seat of our pants* (by our feelings and intuitions), and ignore our instruments, everyone onboard could be killed. The mind is a very powerful force and tries to fool you in the clouds. We practiced with an instructor as our co-pilot and a hood to block our vision outside the cockpit to simulate being in the clouds. Because of the vibrations and lights flickering through the rotor blades, your inner ear gets fooled into believing you are in a turn, or sometimes it even feels like you are actually flying inverted, which a helicopter cannot do. Even so, the tendency is to adjust the controls to compensate for that feeling. So you turn left to roll out of what feels like a steep right turn, and unintentionally put yourself into a steep left turn because you were actually flying straight and level as your instruments indicated. So we *force ourselves, against our feelings*, to believe our instruments. Sometimes it takes looking up from under the hood and out the window to see if we are actually flying straight and level. As soon as we see the horizon as our True reference, the feeling goes away. But in a real life scenario, flying in the clouds with that very strong physical feeling of being inverted or in a steep bank, we cannot look out the window for our reference point. So we must have faith in our instruments and *resist the forces of nature and intuition that try to fool us.*

The same happens in life when we go inside our *Self* and consult our feelings and intuition about what is right and wrong. Again, the mind is very powerful and tries to fool us with other influences, pressures and false references around us. We may think or feel we are doing good, and helping our *Self* and others in life, but like being in the clouds at 10,000 feet without our instruments to keep us flying straight and level, our feelings and intuition will often be wrong. This is the value of our *True North* in navigation and in life. In critical situations it can save our life, or at a minimum, keep us on course. It gives us the appropriate course correction in every perspective of life to insure we achieve our desired result.

Chapter 5: True North of American Values

If you believe in God and the American values system, your *True North* is most likely God and the Bible like it was for the Founding Fathers of our country. Even the well known and openly anti-religious Founding Father, Thomas Paine, who was a deist (believing in God as the Creator but remaining inactive in our lives), believed in the values and principles of the Bible and actively studied them. He said, "*Man cannot make, or invent, or contrive principles; he can only discover them; and he ought to look through the discovery to the Author.*"

The Founding Fathers incorporated God and the Bible into the Declaration of Independence, Constitution and Bill of Rights of the United States, and clearly intended America to be a God-centered, Judeo-Christian nation with the Bible as its *True North*. Whether or not you know or believe anything about God and the Bible, everyone is born with a conscience that is our innate understanding of right and wrong. The Bible tells us this through the story of Adam and Eve who ate from the *Tree of the Knowledge of Good and Evil*. So at the basic level of *True North* values and principles, whether you believe God created us with conscience, or we evolved with conscience, our conscience is there to help us understand right from wrong, good from evil. It is one of our *instruments* for navigating life. Beyond conscience, nearly everyone in America at its founding was educated in the Bible as their primary *instrument* of *True North* for navigating life. The need and application for the Bible never went away, but the secular left has always been threatened by the notion that there is anyone or anything greater than man and his capacity to reason. This thinking is analogous to *flying by the seat of your pants*, and ending up inverted in the clouds without knowing it. Christian and Jewish believers today still believe we must educate ourselves from a source beyond the knowledge, intuition and feelings of man. That source, and primary *instrument* in the flying analogy, is the Bible. Jews and Christians believe the Bible is the inspired Word of God, the inerrant and infallible *Truth*. It is True, *Truth*. Not just true to you, and others have a different *Truth*. It is the final and complete *Truth*. The *Truth* by which all men are judged.

Chapter 6: True North of Secular America
The loud minority leadership in America that I referenced previously is largely a secular group of Americans who look to drive God and the Bible out of society. Their True *Truth*, not just true to them, but they believe to be true to everyone, is *knowledge, power, control, social justice, interdependence, fairness and equality*. They do not look to a higher power than man for *knowledge* and *power* to *control* society and bring about *social justice*, *interdependence*, *fairness and equality* of individuals, groups and nations of the world. Leaders in America with a secular *True North* may be a minority, but they have a strong influence, and may in fact become the majority voice in America, because they target large groups based on race, class and gender to adopt their secular values and principles. Their strategy is to divide and conquer by exploiting racial, class and gender inequality in America and pursuing social and economic equality for all. This exploitation strategy happens with blacks, Latinos, illegal immigrants, the poor, the middle class, gays and unmarried women in America under the auspices of social and economic justice. *Honesty* and *integrity* do not often accompany these pursuits, because to those with a secular *True North*, the ends justify the means for *social justice and equality*. In *True North* of God and the Bible, there is only *equal justice,* with clear and contrary positions on *fairness* and *collective equality* of individuals,

groups and nations. Those who believe in free market capitalism and American Exceptionalism inspired by God-given *individual liberties* and the pursuit of happiness and *prosperity* are the opponents of those with a secular *True North*.

Sexual freedom however, is the one individual liberty they demand, and is contrary to the values and principle of God and the Bible. A secularist approach, with nothing to judge and condemn their "moral truths," is the only way to justify sexual promiscuity, same-sex or gender-neutral lifestyles, and ridding themselves of unwanted consequences such as the life of a baby for the freedom to have sex under any circumstance they choose.

Chapter 7: Truth in your True North

The Truth we have discussed so far is a *True North* kind of *Truth* regarding values and principles. *Truth* to someone with a *True North* of God and the Bible, is going to be very different than *Truth* to someone with a secular *True North* as just described. *Truth* is therefore relative to our defining values and principles that vary between individuals, groups and nations. Defining *True North* for our character as an individual, group and nation, is so critical for this reason.

There are two other essential truths to building a strong foundation for character: The truth of *honesty* and the truth of *reality*. *Honesty* is being true <u>to</u> your *Self*, the *World*, and your *True North*. *Reality* is being true <u>in</u> your *Self*, the *World*, and your *True North*. *Real* truth doesn't have an agenda. It is the factual true or false, yes or no, black or white, information around us. It is *reality* about you, your *True North*, and other people and things in the *World*.

True North is the strongest anchor point of your Character Pyramid. It is the point that faces into the wind of an oncoming storm. It must be *real,* and you must be *honest* in your *True North* to establish a firm foundation in character. This may be the first time you have thought consciously about your guiding values and principles in life. Do you have a definite source for your guiding values and principles? If it is not yet *real* for you, you must make it your objective to gain knowledge in, and decide on, your *True North*. You must make it *real*. If it is not *real*, it is not *true*, and it will not be your anchor in a storm.

Then when you have made your *True North* real, you must have *honesty* with your *Self* about your *True North*. If you decide your *True North* is God and the Bible, but live by secular values, you are not being *honest* with your *Self* and the *World*. If you decide on a secular *True North*, what is the source of your values and are they *real* and clearly defined? If *collective equality* for you or your group is your *True North*, are you *honest* with your *Self* and others that this is your aim? If you tell yourself and others that American Judeo-Christian values from the Declaration and Constitution are the values our country and you should live by, but you have established a secular *True North* as the anchor point of your Character Pyramid, then you are not being *honest* and *true* to yourself and others. In the face of a storm, your Character Pyramid will come unmoored and be set adrift, subject to any course the strongest winds and waves will take you. A strong character has its foundation in *Truth* (*reality* and *honesty*) about your *True North* guiding values and principles to weather any storm.

Similar to Dr. Robert Hartman's axiom about *good* being anything that fulfills the concept of something (containing all the properties of a particular person place or thing; a good chair or a good thief), Truth in regard to your principles and values has an axiom of its own, being *the ideas that fulfill the concept of your ideology* (one's *True North*).

So if a *leader of character* from Group 2 adopts the ideology that *equality for all* is better than *individual prosperity*, then his axiom of Truth is any statement or idea that fulfills his ideology of *collective fairness and equality over individual prosperity*. This is how a leader from Group 2 values people and things (his value system), which in turn defines how he thinks and makes decisions. This kind of Truth stems from his *True North* ideology or value system.

Because the *True North* values and principles of a Group 1 leader of character are in opposition to Group 2 values and principles, Truth to these two categories of leaders will also be different. For Group 1 leaders, *individual prosperity* achieved through honesty and integrity is virtuous. *Collective equality and fairness* can only be obtained by holding down, or taking from, those who have achieved prosperity, and redistributing prosperity to those who have not achieved it. To someone who values *individual achievement and prosperity, collective fairness and equality* violate their *Truth* of *honesty and integrity*, and shows weakness of character in both the individual and the nation that promotes these values.

America today is divided on values and principles (the American *True North*) and as a result the American Character is weakened, as is our force for good in the world. We as individuals in America are electing leaders of our nation who have a secular *True North* and are not honest about it. They tell us they support the American Values System of the Declaration and Constitution, but they proceed with their secular *True North* values and in fact push God and the Bible out of every facet of America and threaten our individual rights and liberties. Their words are not in alignment with their deeds and their character is counter to the American Character of our Forefathers who fought and died for the American Values System of the Declaration of Independence and Constitution of the United States. The good news is that we have the history and record as the most prosperous nation on earth, and the power and strength of individual character, to nullify the course corrections attempted by leaders with a secular *True North*. We do this by reinforcing our personal *True North* in American Values and promoting individual liberty and prosperity, which will strengthen the American Character to once again become the greatest force for good in the world. It happens one individual at a time through the power of *Wisdom*.

Chapter 8: What is Wisdom

Individuals and groups in America have lost sight of what is truly good and bad, right and wrong. Without a final truth from anything greater than the feelings and opinions of man, all truth is relative to what you believe, and in a true democracy (which America is truly not), the majority prevails, whether right or wrong, just as in a dictatorship, the dictator prevails, whether right or wrong. In this case, there is no *true* right or wrong; just what the majority or the dictator considers right or wrong.

If this is correct, we are back at the problem Dr. Robert Hartman faced in Nazi Germany, where through twisted manipulation of the truth, evil was inverted to appear good, but many of that era *felt* like they were flying straight and level. When you are inverted but unaware and without instruments for a *true* reference, a climb out of the clouds will bury you into the ground, upside-down. In the clutter and confusion, the flicker of lights, and the pressures and stress of life, bad can *feel* good, and good can *feel* bad to individuals, groups and even whole nations that fly without *instruments*. That's why we must *believe our instruments* and resist the false feelings of a turn or inversion when our *instruments* tell us we are flying true. That is why we cannot go inside our *Self* and think or do what our emotions tell us when we have *instruments* to give us *True* perspective. That is why we need a *True North* that is clearly defined in writing and can be consulted visually like the horizon when it feels like we are in a steep turn. We need *instruments* to tell us and show us what is *real*.

Dr. Hartman left us another *instrument* of navigation not based in feelings, opinions, history, or faith, but an *instrument* based in *logic* and supported by math and science. He left us *formal axiology,* an *instrument* for measuring value in people, things and ideas. Because of his work, we have, in addition to *conscience* and *True North*, another *instrument* to check when something *feels* wrong or *feels* right to see if we are in fact climbing or descending. In the case of *individual ethics*, is it right or wrong; in *social ethical matters,* does it make things better or worse; in *economics,* is there profit or loss; concerning *technology,* is there more or less benefit; and in the case of our Character Pyramid, is there *Wisdom* or lack of *Wisdom*?

Knowledge vs. Wisdom

So far in defining and building our Character Pyramid, we have addressed the facets of *Truth* and *True North*. *Truth* of *Self*, the *World*, and your *True North* can also be described as knowledge. Knowledge is an accumulation of thoughts and ideas that may be important, but have little value until applied in a *practical* or *personal* way. Knowledge is therefore *potential* power. It has the potential for good or for bad depending on how it is applied. *Wisdom* is *True* power and insures knowledge of the *World* and your *Self* becomes a force for good and not bad.

Wisdom adds *value; value* has *meaning; meaning* leads to *Purpose.* *Wisdom* in the Character Pyramid is represented by the framework coming from the three anchor points of *True North*, *Self*, and *World*, to the top point of the pyramid, representing *Purpose* (Figure 5).

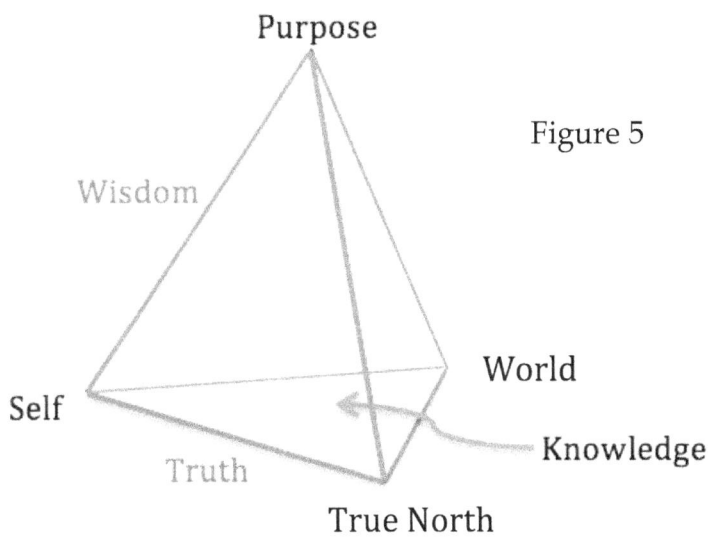

Figure 5

Wisdom, applied to a base of *Truth,* gives dimension to the Character Pyramid, adding *value, meaning*, and *Purpose* to our lives. The greater the *Wisdom*, the greater the *value*, and more *meaningful* our *Purpose*. This applies to an individual, group or nation. So how do we get *Wisdom* and apply it to *Truth* of *Self*, the *World* and our *True North*?

*Wisdom is adding value
by knowing what is truly good from bad,
and making things better*

In formal axiology, the axiom of *good* is anything that fulfills its concept or properties, and *not good* or *bad* is anything that does not. Further, a person, thing or idea has value to the degree that it has properties. In other words, the more properties something has to define it, the richer and more valuable it is. We are good and add value by living up to the characteristics of a good husband, wife, boss or friend for example. Our relationships are richer when we are a better husband, wife, boss or friend by fulfilling more *good* properties. We have the same opportunity to lose value and make things worse by taking away good characteristics from something, someone or ourselves. <u>*Wisdom* only adds value by knowing what is truly good from bad and making things better, not worse</u>. As it relates to the Character Pyramid, *Wisdom* points up toward the top of the pyramid, which adds value. *Wisdom* is lacking when we de-value someone or something and move down the pyramid. There are three *dimensions of value* in formal axiology and *three levels of Wisdom* in the Character Pyramid, designating a *hierarchy of value and Wisdom*. We have the ability to add value or take it away but *Wisdom only adds value*. We will understand *Wisdom* better, by understanding Dr. Hartman's three *dimensions of value*.

The three dimensions of value working from lowest to highest in value are

Structured Value ■ , *Practical Value* ○ , and *Personal Value* ♡ . The Character Pyramid with its *hierarchy of value and Wisdom* in shown in Figure 6.

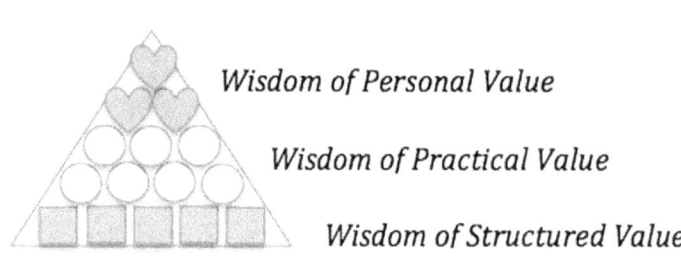

Figure 6

Structured Value has a symbol of a square representing *structured thinking in the box*. *Structured Value* is present in our beliefs, principles, ideas and definitions of our *Self* and the *World*. It is our knowledge and the conclusions we draw from that knowledge. Our concept of a man or woman, a pencil, and the formula for the area of a rectangle are examples of *Structured Value*. *Structured value* is generally true or false, existent or non-existent. You are a man or woman. It is a pencil or it is not. There are no shades of grey in *Structured Value*. It is either the formula for a rectangle or it is not. Even though *Structured Value* is the lowest in the *hierarchy of value and Wisdom*, it is extremely important and forms the foundation of all higher *Practical* and *Personal Value* of people, things and concepts in our life. *Structured Value* is the base upon which we build greater value. The U.S Constitution and Declaration of Independence are concepts of *Structured Value* that form our foundation as a country to build upon in *practical* and *personal* ways.

Practical Value has a symbol of a circle representing the practical *worldview*. *Practical Value* involves real-world comparisons of people, things and *Self*, as well as practical and societal roles, positions, actions and results. *Practical Value* exists in the physical realm of the senses rather than the conceptual realm of the mind, like *Structured Value*. If *Structured Value* is the <u>What</u> in life, *Practical Value* is the <u>How</u>. It is the real-world, hands-on *doing* of tasks, and taking action *in* and *on* the <u>What</u> in our life.

It follows then that *Personal Value* is the <u>Why</u> in life. *Personal Value* is the highest *dimension of value* and has a symbol of a heart representing *people*, *feelings* and the *human passion and spirit*. *Empathy* and *intuition* are encompassed in *Personal Value*. *Uniqueness* and *rarity* are also characteristic of *Personal Value* in the same way rarity in diamonds is a function of their high value. *Personal Value transcends time and space* with *infinite emotional and spiritual value* that makes it difficult to describe in words and put a practical value on. Because of this, *Practical Value* offers the greatest potential for good by fulfilling the infinite and intangible characteristics that define it.

In our life, we have the opportunity to see our *Self* and the *World* in light of the three *dimensions of value*. Let me share a personal example.

A Girl on the Beach

I was stationed in the Hawaii for 4 years when I was 24 years old and a lieutenant in the Army. Waikiki Beach was always packed with tourists on vacation, and a good place to hang out on the weekend. One day I saw a girl on the beach who captured my attention and compelled me to want to meet her. She didn't look like a tourist but I couldn't tell for sure. I was not accustomed to walking up to girls I didn't know on the beach, but all day I looked for an opportunity to casually start a conversation and meet her. It turned out I waited too long and she picked up her things and left. I kicked myself for missing the chance to meet her.

Three weeks later I went back to the same beach in the same spot hoping maybe to see the same girl again if she was not a tourist. To my happiness and surprise she was there again. This time I strategically positioned my chair to give myself a better opportunity to meet her. It took most of the day, but I finally mustered the courage to introduce myself. I had overheard her name three weeks prior so that gave me an opening to break the ice. We talked the rest of the afternoon, and she did in fact live and work in Hawaii. To make a long story very short, we went on a date two days later and that was 27 years ago. We just celebrated our 25th Anniversary and have two daughters.

The Hierarchy of Value

Let's observe the three *dimensions of value* in this story. Before going to the beach, I had a *concept in my mind* of the type of girl I was attracted to and interested in meeting. The girl I saw on the beach that first day fulfilled the *concept in my mind* the minute I saw her. It was the *true or false concept* that constitutes *Structured Value*. We had no interaction so the value I held for her initially took place *only in my mind*. We both were wearing dark sunglasses so it was not apparent that we were even looking in each other's direction. We laid in the sun, went swimming and had no contact before she got up and left. Everything observable was pretty black and white, existent or non-existent. If everything had ended that day, the girl I saw on the beach would *only be a memory* (this is *Structured Value*).

On the less obvious side, there were plenty of *sensory observations* being made the first day I saw her, and she gained significant *Practical Value* with me. I noticed her blonde hair, tan skin and white two-piece suit. She was physically fit and likely an athlete. When I finally got the nerve to approach her, I learned she was a biology teacher and a track coach. As we talked, she gained more *Practical Value* because she fulfilled many more properties I had for a good person and surpassed all comparisons to girls I had met and known previously.

As we dated, our relationship grew richer and deeper, and I valued her at the highest level of *Personal Value,* realizing she could one day be my wife. I knew this because I liked everything about her including the smallest, most insignificant things. I have always had a difficult time describing exactly what I love about her. Love is intangible and the most precious and valuable aspect of Personal Value; a value beyond infinite space and time.

***Seeing and understanding the three dimensions of value in your life,
and their hierarchy of significance and meaning, is the Wisdom of the Character Pyramid***

The same three dimensions of value can even be found in an inanimate object. Take the pencil I am writing with for example. It is a pencil defined by a general but *structured* definition being made of wood, having a point with lead and an eraser. As it rests on my desk, it has *Structured Value.* When I pick it up and use it to write this book, it gains *Practical Value.* It is sharp and dull and all variations in between at times. It is camouflage green with a white eraser. It is my favorite pencil because it feels good in my hand and erases without smudging. These are all points off *Practical Value.*

The most compelling reason <u>why</u> *this* pencil is my favorite pencil however, is because it has *Personal Value* since my daughter gave it to me and it reminds me of her when I see and use it. All my pens and pencils have *Structured* and *Practical Value*, but I use and value *this* pencil more than all others because of its *Personal Value*.

Wisdom is seeing good and bad in the light of *Structured, Practical, and Personal Value* and <u>adding value</u> whenever possible. The three *dimensions of value* combine in our life to make things good or bad, better or worse. For example, I can use my pencil to write a book or to stab and kill someone. In both cases I am using a pencil of *Structured Value* for *practical* purposes (to write or to kill). <u>*Wisdom is knowing good from bad, and making things better not worse*</u>.

Which is better, using my pencil to write a book or to stab and kill someone? I'm sure you see the positive *Practical Value* in writing a book, but what if I saved my family's life by stabbing a home intruder with my pencil? In this case, the *Personal Value* of saving my family's life trumps any *Practical Value* from writing a book. This illustrates the importance of *Truth* made earlier. If some of the facts are not clear or have been distorted, we can be confused about what is good and evil. If our *True North* is not *clearly* aligned with the hierarchy of value that protecting our life and our family with deadly force is at the top of the pyramid, we may in fact lose our life in the above example. We need the *instruments* of our *conscience*, our *True North*, and the *hierarchy of value and Wisdom* to be our reference point for recognizing good and evil.

In formal axiology, everything concerning our *Self*, the *World* and *True North* can be viewed in combinations of the three *dimensions of value*. These combinations can be positive (for good) or negative (for bad). *Wisdom is knowing the direction of good is always up*. We know the highest *dimension of value* is *Personal Value* which must be supported by *Practical Value* grounded in a foundation of *Structured Value* as shown in the Character Pyramid below. (Figure 7)

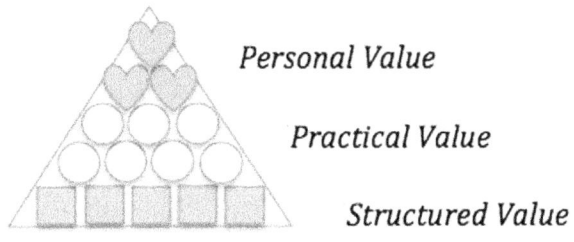

Figure 7

All three dimensions must be present and in their proper *hierarchy of value* or our Character Pyramid is weakened. If we reverse the order, or have a weak foundation in *Structured Value*, or don't support *Personal Value* ♥ with *Practical Value* ○, the Character Pyramid will collapse under pressure. This is what is illustrated in Figure 8 below. This Character Pyramid lacks *Practical Value* ○ (reality) and puts *Structured Value* ■ (policy) over *Practical* ○ (results) and *Personal* Value ♥ (people).

Figure 8

Whether intentional or unintentional, we tend to jumble up our Character Pyramids in life. We have natural preferences and tendencies to one value over another and tend to *over-value* some while *under-valuing* others. It is a function of how clearly we think under various conditions of attention or inattention. In the next chapter you will learn about the six thinking centers in our brain and your own natural thinking pattern. *Wisdom* of *Self* involves knowing your natural thinking talents and non-talents and recognizing the *hierarchy of value* and its significance in your life.

Wisdom also involves recognizing negative (bad) combinations of the three *dimensions of value*. When we devalue people and things, there is a reverse hierarchy to the *dimensions of value* in which *Personal Value* 🤍 is on the bottom designating the worst devaluations 🖤 (Figure 9). This tells us that <u>negative combinations</u> of *Personal Value* are worse than <u>negative combinations</u> of *Practical* and *Structured Value*. Example: Breaking your leg (of *Personal Value*) is worse than breaking a pencil (of *Structured and Practical Value*).

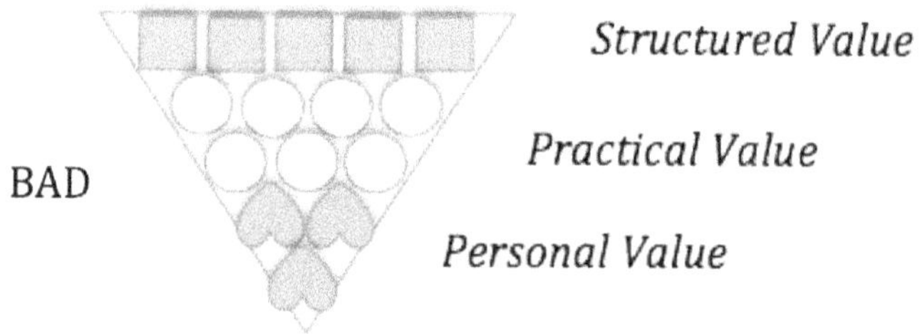

BAD — *Structured Value* / *Practical Value* / *Personal Value*

Figure 9

When facing the *good* and *bad* of everyday life, *Wisdom* is knowing which way is up and maintaining a steady climb.

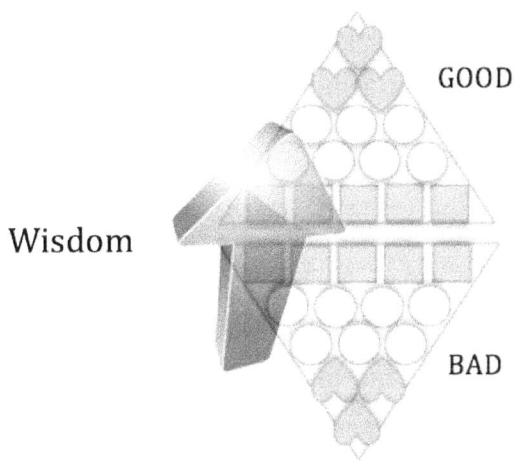

The fall of Lance Armstrong

Lance Armstrong recently admitted to the world that he lied and in fact used performance-enhancing drugs to win his seven Tour de France races. My understanding is that he raised approximately $450 million for cancer research over the years and his personal net worth is approximately $100 million. Was the lie worth the benefits that resulted?

There are various combinations of *Structured*, *Practical*, and *Personal Value* in this scenario, and I don't know all the details, but to apply the basic principles of formal axiology, here is what I see:

1. Armstrong cheated (devaluation of *Structured Value* – law and policy)
2. Armstrong perpetuated the lie through a cover-up of false testimony (devaluation of *Practical Value* – his words and deeds were deceiving and have lost all credibility and meaning)
3. Armstrong destroyed the career of people who knew the truth, but whose character and credibility he had to attack and destroy to hide his own false character (devaluation of *Personal Value*)
4. Armstrong destroyed his own *personal* character by betraying everyone in his life including his fans and those who looked up to him for hope, strength and courage. He cannot be trusted (devaluation of *Personal Value*)
5. If Armstrong's *True North* is God and the Bible, he clearly acted in opposition to the *Truths* about stealing, bearing false witness, and coveting what was not his. In addition, all of these devaluations have deeper secondary and tertiary degradation of *Personal Value* against himself, other people, and God)

The entire ordeal is a devaluation of *Structured* ↘ , *Practical* ↘ and most devastatingly his own *Personal Value* ↘ and that of people who trusted him, defended him, and found strength in him. Any logic that *Practical Value* gained ↗ by Armstrong lying and cheating, offsets the damage of *Personal Value* against himself and other people ↘ , goes against the *Wisdom* of the Character Pyramid and cannot be reconciled.

Further, some people may argue that lives were saved ↗ with the money raised for cancer research, but there is no telling the lives would *not* have been saved if Lance Armstrong did not lie and cheat his way to victory, fame and fortune. Measured with the *Wisdom of Structured, Practical and Personal Value* there was far more severe and deep devaluation of *Personal Value* ↘ that outweighs any *Practical Value* ↗ or other potential value that might have resulted from his deception. By the *Wisdom* of the Character Pyramid, the ends do not justify the means.

With the aid of your own *conscience* and *True North*, *Wisdom* to know if you are climbing toward good or descending toward evil becomes even more clear.

Chapter 9: Knowledge and Wisdom of Self

Knowledge of *Self* is the second anchor of your Character Pyramid (Figure 10) and begins with knowing how you *value* your *Self*, and people and things in the *World*.

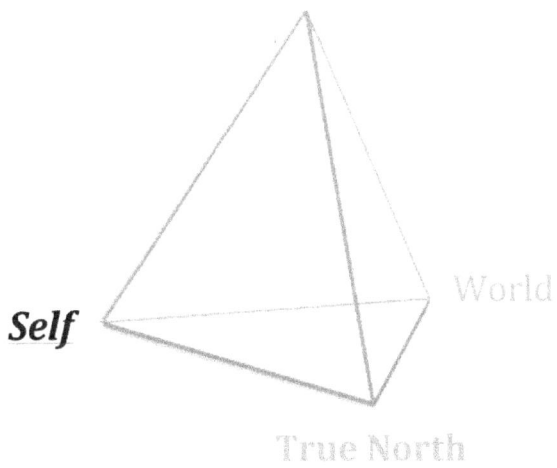

Figure 10

We have six thinking centers in our brain corresponding to *Structured, Practical* and *Personal Value*, relative to *Self* and the *World*. Those six thinking centers are depicted below.

Your Six Thinking Centers

Personal World
Empathy
Compassion
Passion
Personal Intuition

Personal Self
Your Own Feelings
Your Dignity
Your Loves
Who You Are
You on the Inside

Practical World
The Social World
Results - ROI
Practical Thinking
Better – Best
People in Politics
Energy - Power

Practical Self
Your Body
Your Roles
What You Do
Your Capabilities
How You Compare
Your Skills

Structured World
Right-Wrong
Laws
Concepts
Understanding
Logic
Predictable
Authority

Structured Self
Personal Values
Self Expectations
Self Shoulds
Values
Standards
Self Definition

Parietal Lobe
Frontal Lobe
Occipital Lobe
Temporal Lobe
Cerebellum
Brain Stem

Copyright, Clear Direction, Inc., Dallas, TX

We all have natural preferences to the thinking centers we use most and best, which in turn give us our unique *natural thinking talents*. Through formal axiology we can identify those preferences and measure how well we naturally value things and people including our *Self*, in each thinking center.

Your thinking preferences and ability to value create a consistent and automatic thinking pattern that gives you natural talents and non-talents. You may or may not be aware of these patterns and talents, but an axiology assessment will tell you your *natural thinking pattern,* and your *top thinking talents*. This is an invaluable tool for understanding how you value in terms of *Structured, Practical* and *Personal Value*. It is a starting point of knowledge about your Self that forms the base of your Character Pyramid.

As a bonus for buying and reading this book, you can take our assessment for free (a $250 value) and in 10 minutes, have your Personal Talent Profile in a 15-page report full of valuable information to start building your Character Pyramid. You will find the assessment link in Appendix 1.

When you begin to know and understand your *Self* better, people and things have more meaning in your life. You see the Wisdom in expanding your knowledge in *practical* and *personal* ways that create more *value* and *meaning* in your life and the lives of others, which clarifies your *Purpose*. You will gain *Wisdom* and see the *hierarchy of value* from *knowledge* to *practical* application to the highest *Personal Value*. Your natural thinking pattern operates in automatic mode and will get you by even if unaware of it, but when you become more *Self-*aware, the *Wisdom* of the *hierarchy of value* brings another dimension to your life and your potential is unbound.

We started this book with the observation that there is a character deficit among leaders in America, and our American Character, supported by American Values in the Declaration of Independence and Constitution, is at risk of being inverted, or at least set on a very different course. It is up to us as individuals of this great country to firmly establish our individual character by strengthening our own Character Pyramid in *Truth* and *Wisdom* of our *Self*, the *World*, and our *True North*. Our family Character Pyramid is next in importance, and if everyone starts there, the Character of our nation will be restored to the American Values System that our Founding Fathers established, as *one nation, under God, indivisible, with liberty and justice, for all*.

Chapter 10: Building Your Character Pyramid

Character to me, is everything in a leader. Character involves *Truth* and *Wisdom* about *Self*, the *World* around you, and your *True North* guiding values and principles in life. Without *Truth* a leader has no *character*. He is fooling himself as much as he is trying to fool others. Without *Wisdom* a leader has no *character*. Knowledge from books and school is important, but without the *Wisdom of Structured, Practical and Personal Value*, knowledge does not account for much in life. You have come a long way to gaining *Truth* and *Wisdom* in your life if you have read and understood the principles shared in this book *and* your *Personal Talent Profile*. This is an ongoing process in life and one that you will benefit from the more it is applied to your personal and professional life. You also have the opportunity to offer this information and perspective to others in your life including family and friends. If you would like to continue the process of developing your *Purpose* in life through *Truth* and *Wisdom* of *Self*, the *World*, and your *True North*, please visit our website at www.TalentProsIntl.com and click on the coaching menu. We offer online coaching programs as well as group and individual coaching by phone and in-person. We also have special events such as hunting and sailing adventure weekends with other like-minded Americans. Thank you for investing your time and talent in your own success, and the success and longevity of our country. Future generations will thank us, as we thank those who came before us.

Please be at liberty to pass this e-book and assessment link to anyone you know, to help them understand the *dimensions of value*, the *hierarchy of Wisdom* and the importance to revitalize our American Values and strengthen our American Character. The world needs a strong America now, more than ever.

Appendix 1

Online link for Bonus Axiology Assessment:
CharacterDeficit.TalentProsIntl.com

www.ingramcontent.com/pod-product-compliance
Lightning Source LLC
Chambersburg PA
CBHW071800170526
45167CB00003B/1113